# A Doe Licking Dew
# off Tiger Lilies

# A Doe Licking Dew off Tiger Lilies

JUDITH SOLT

**To order additional copies of this book, contact:**
Xlibris
1-888-795-4274
www.Xlibris.com
Orders@Xlibris.com
813429

# CONTENTS

# Rococo

Eighteenth century man and woman porcelain figurines.

On the shelf.
Behind glass.
Safe.
Protected.

Never gone anywhere, not really here.

Dusted.
Washed.
*Never aging.*
Hollow.
Cool.

Positioned close, never touching.

Always doing, never finalizing anything.

Sightless staring.
Pink, Blue, White.

Curtsey.
Smile.
Bow.

What do they say for themselves?

"We have never made a mistake."

# X

1)   I spoke, I expressed an idea.
she continued taking as
though I hadn't said a word.  I
wondered if I spoke?

2)   He walked by, he eyes didn't blink or turn
he focused on something behind.  My face
and head.

3)   As a child I was in a shop with my mother it
was the first time I saw a fossil.
I felt sorrowful.
Crying, my mother took me to the car.
The fossil made a visual record for always. I felt old and
tired when asked all I could say. "I want to go home"

4)   The tour guide at Mesa
Verde pointed out a hand print a
child place there when the cliff
dwellers built their dwellings.

5)   On the list of people, who
came on the ship with my
ancestors some passengers made
X (his mark).

I *marveled* at that!

# Phillis

When I think of phillis I see a young mare
romping in the meadow coming
to the fence looking  with
puzzlement, a cocked head No
concept of limitation.
*I call her Philly.*
I had committed myself to the asylum.

She drove me to a house I had selected from a list.
The rug, green with roses all over it. I
knew I was in the wrong place.

The living room walls were lined with discarded people,
reduced to vegetables. Propped and tied in flowered,
stuffed chairs.

In the kitchen, the woman put coffee in front of us and
kept telling me how upset I was.

Her handyman was muscular and mustached; he
lifted and feed the bodies. he kept offering me wine
and smiling, asking me over and over if I was going
to live there. The kind of man who thinks *no* means
*yes*.

As the woman and I left the bedroom, she showed me she
offered me a tranquilizer.

I said nothing my head  became rigid.
I could only see in front of me. I
some how managed walking.

Filly was at my side going to the car.
With each stride we made, across the lawn my body
became flexible.

I felt my mother's grip around my body.    *Break*

# Lilith

She was made from the same earth as Adam.
His first wife.
He wanted to dominate her.
She left to live in the desert, refusing.

Eve was crested from Adam's rib.
She put her man first.
She will be everything he thinks a woman *ought to be*.
All aspects of cleaning up after him.
Eve has influenced world culture, for a long time.

My mother worked hard to be.
Eve. Meek, submissive.
"Whatever you want is fine", "dear".
Sometimes

An object would fly from the kitchen with piercing screams
Mother, wife, secretary, cook, cleaner, laundress, bill payer,
strong objections to impossible expectations.
Lilith would surface. Descending on her
children making them more vulnerable
than herself.

My great grandmother stomped her foot through the
floor of the porch, her son had run off with a hired girl.

Aunt Lidia's husband had to justify deforcing her "She was
too independent" Everyone agreed. I did *not*.

Her job was to pass out pay checks to migrant workers.
"Those rough sort of people."
She smoked.  Her car had a rumble seat.

When I feel vulnerable or afraid of dependency.
I look around for Lilith.
When I found her I came alive. *I found my mouth!*


I was furious and thought *not me!*
None of that boring .
Adam and Eve stuff .
I don't accept  dominance.

Dominance is Fascism.

## The Dunes

I drove from the elbow out the cape.
I was looking for the dunes, I had seen as a child.
There were no longer signs.
    They were not on the maps.

The park ranger told us the dunes move forty feet a year.
Always shifting temperature and pressure produce a
moaning. The old road was covered.  As I drove beside a
pond I could hear and see the dune filling it.

It felt as though it could cover my tracks my body my life.
There would be no written record no longer a memory or
thought of me. My name,

Less
Then a silent sound.

# Hours Days Years

When I heard Jesus's story.

I wanted to live next door, be a casual friend of him and his family

To be with Daniel in the furnace and not burn.

To call with Jesus in a loud voice "Lazarus, come forth."

Watch him walk out of death.

I agree with Thomas.

Hours, days, years spent Sunday mornings reading stories from the Bible.

One dreary story lecture lesson following in an endless line. That was when I started to overeat.

The Bible oozing down over my eyes, closing my ears

in my mouth   squeezing my stomach.

I ate the church, stone by stone.
Tried to horde all the blood for myself.

## My Face

Someone tell my mother my face hurts

 Held back tears are in the muscles.

Rage in the bones.

A hard crusted mask of terror has collected under the skin.

I am opening my face, freeing it from the unconscious,
asleep, denial faces that have passed me all my life.


I want to see with my whole face.

It wants to breathe.

I want my face to feel like a landscape.

## Jonathan Cox

He called himself an archaeologist. I
doubt he pushed a shovel into the soil.

He demanded his assistant get marry.
He never did.

They rode through the countryside, collecting
everything.

In cement monoliths he covered all the wall, ceiling, and
floor with tiles. Depicting stories from the Old Testament.

On the tour of his house,
I was anticipating beauty in his bedroom.

I walked across the room carefully leaned over his bed
there was one thin line of tile. The last tile made clear
the depiction.
I turned to my friend standing in the doorway.

"Blue beard?"

## We Will Pray for You

"You are not seasoned to be in our company."
      EVERY GROUPING OF EVERYTHING, ON THE
    PLANET EARTH IS BASICALLY
    THE SAME.
      NO TWO INDIVIDUAL ARE IDENTICAL.
"Unclean: you are living outside of god's acceptance."
      OFF THE ARCTIC COAST
      A GLACIER IS IN A PERPETUAL MOVE OF
      FALLING INTO THE OCEAN
      IN RHYTHM TO THE PULSE OF
      THE EARTH
"We will show you all your imperfections."
      THERE ARE MORE CELLS IN OUR BRAINS
    THAN STARES IN THE SKY.
"Your path is wrong. We will show you *the way*"
      DECIDED AT CREATION, THE EXACT
      VIBRATION NEEDED. TO MAINTAIN THE
      ORBITAL FLOW OF EVERYTHING
      WITH MUSIC.
"Your blemishes are miniscule.We will cut and sear them out
                    Of your skin."
      EACH STAR, PLANET, MOON AND THE
      ASTEROID BELT DEBRIS HAS ITS OWN ORBIT.
  "We have to change and control you."
      WE ALL STARTED FROM STAR DUST.

# November Rose

The day before thanksgiving my sister's baby died.

Mom went to Denver to be with her.

The grieving mother sprinkled water on the baby's head.

Committed her soul to God.

Knowing she would die.

In the dark my cousin and I went for a walk.

 I would have preferred dusk.

My cousin was reluctant to be with me.

I picked the last rose.

It lasted an unusually long time.

Down is down
Dead is dead
Gone is gone

I witnessed an evergreen downed.
A sensation of motion.
Wild life escaping in a frenzy.
Their babies left behind.

Wood splitting, snapping.

The vibration hard, loud, heavy until I
could feel it in my body. All of the
mountain side, repeating the trauma.

A small rise as though it were breathing one
last sigh.

Still.  Silent.

One field after another of dead soldiers
                        Far as I could see.

We can't bring them back.

Inspired by: the Joy Luck Club Amy Tan
## Let's Share

Putting together a small part of my mother's story
while I agonizingly wrenched out my truth.
She compulsively told everyone else's story; one story after
another without a pause, desperate to control the moment.
They were rehearsed.
Telling little of herself.
   In *her* mind I had no stories to tell.
I was always reaching out to her.
I did not realize I was saying good bye.
She was constantly leaving.
Now she is gone.

## This Tree

All its seed fallen on asphalt.

A breeze rustles dried out leaves,
overhead still on the branches.

I grieve for my unborn children.

Some seed is carried on the wind.

Planting a different kind of seed.

Carried in my heart.

# Family Anthology

1.

My father's mother was a girl her father took her to a farmhouse to see the bedroom, where an axe murder had taken place. The murdered couple was my mother's great aunt and uncle. My grandmother slept with her father for a while, too afraid to sleep alone.

2.

My father was a boy, he slept with his widowed ant. Once they woke to fine the snow drifted over them from the open window.

3.

Taking my mother for a walk my grandmother saw my father in the school play yard. He had tied my mother's brother to a tree.

4.

When my father was not home I slept with my mother. When my mother was not home I slept with my father.

## White Fluffy Stuff

I was five, when I died in my fathers bed.

He took me, plucked me out.

An empty milk weed pod
                    With all the white fluffy
                                    stuff gone.

He thought I would forget.


Now, how can I ask this man if
he cares for me without


Dying     again.

## Sheila Lymon

I saw a shadow of the cross cast over Europe.

A Hag gnawed her way through the foundation of the
church.
She went down the road cackling in peals of laughter.
Thinking she was free....

The man who guarded the door, to the old ones locked
it and hanged himself.

Passages that slipped between worlds and time were
forbidden.

Our Mother could not come to us, nurture or protect us.

The only way open to her was through fire.

Given as sacrifices to a punishing god.

We asked the church for bread, he gave us a stone.

## Blame Game

Let's play!
We can blame the Neighbor.
Husband.    Wife.
Dog    or        Cat!
Government.
Mom        Dad

We can let our Children carry the blame.

Women are blamed more than Men.

Blame the last Administration.

It is safer to blame Mom than Dad.

The worst is blaming ourselves.

Oh yes, blame God she/he will still love you.

Most of what I was blamed for had nothing to do with me.
I'm adult now.  Responsible for;   How I Feel
What I Think
Say and how I Say it.
Responsible for my Intentions.

I have the ability to Respond.

# Mystery School

This hawk appears to be enormous.
 He  looks large enough to fill my back yard.
    He is not.
This must be the magic of nature.
Drawing animals on the ceiling and walls of caves were for
empowerment and courage. Help them reclaim their inner
self.  Early humans knew, if they did not overcome their
fears they would not survive.
The Earth Mothers had immense sculptures of themselves
seated on chairs flanked by a carved lioness under
each chair arm.

Here I sit in my psychologist's waiting room.
The legs of the table next to me are enhanced
with bronze stylized lion's feet.

## Shaman Drumming Circle

Carefully selected clothing.
Necklaces and pouch
Old friends, my favorite stones in pockets.
Wrapping my drum in red cloth.
Three sessions of drumming.
To journey.
Flying and weeping.
Faraway  in outer space.
Looking back, my tears spray in an ark
                            covering the earth.

## The Sacrifice  (a dream)

A perfect white ewe lamb
was being given for sacrifice.

Shaven, washed, three legs cut off.


Helplessly it kept trying to stand.

 A priest laid his hand on my shoulder.

"The lamb is you".

# Night Stalker

The bride and groom received witnesses of their wedding on the side lawn under the sycamore tree.

On their honeymoon, in Wyoming, in the dark, on ice, a blizzard.
Their car rolled off the side of the road.

Their graves are a few feet from the sycamore tree.

Several other deaths in our meeting and a three hundred year tradition, between the Mohawk tribe and  Philadelphia Quakers.
Helping each other survive.
My personal grief was too great. To hold the meetings grief.
I invited Chief Jacob Swamp to visit us.

He talked to us about our grief.
Told us of the night stalker. An old man dressed in black with a stick. Traveling at night.  After he struck  a house someone who lived there, would  die.

At night when leaving a friends house alone I could feel it following close, trying to engulf me.

## Possession

Shy, pale, thin girl child.
placid, no emotion, no ides no
expression: dead-eyed calm.
Occasionally someone passes she looks out, numb and
mute.

Formless dress hanging from her shoulders;
Long straight hair, dress, and  face  all the same color.

I bring her forward when I am shocked.
We can sit idle for hours.

I saw her peering out of my left eye.

# Night                    (a dream)

The streets were wet reflecting lights of the closed stores.
The only sound was the click of my heels on the pavement.
I descended into the open cellar door in the sidewalk.

There were naked manikins lined up in the dark.

An old man in a cutaway and white gloves, complained
that they had been waiting a long time.

As each indifferent manikin approached.
I tore a handful of flesh off my body.
and applied it to their sides.
Instantly they had hair, clothes, high heels, and  a purse.
They said nothing and walked out.

The old man told me to look at my self.
My body was stripped down to a skeleton.

A seashell was on the shelf beside my hand.

He whispered,

"Listen."

I heard my own voice reduced to formless garble.

## Natalie and Deon

In my destress!

Trying to comfort me,   a touch. Guarded *my
mother, is in this somehow!*

I find myself renting and
tearing down  this
ancient stone wall.

## About Mother

At the edge of being inside myself.

earning my alone, easy place.

All my selves  come together leaving
the space I need to be me.

She opened the door enough to see her eye.

I hear in my mind the music box playing the
one wound *every day.*

When I entered my room I
knew she had been there.

Then the chair, then the wast paper basket
adjusted slightly to be in the way. She
whispered, "Want company?" Something
in my body folded.


I invited her in.

## The Mind Will Make it Real

Four months, lying awake.
I know, *I will sleep to night.*

A weight on  the side of my bed.

Sleepily I turned my head to see a demon. Sitting there
swinging his legs He asked me. "You want to play?"
I knew immediately he was created from guilt. My fathers
guilt.  I had taken on.

He had long hair over  all his body, a set of horns from his
neck that went to the top of his head.

I rolled my head back on my pillow, for a brief moment I
thought of looking to see if he was still there.  My heart
pounded rapidly.  I thought it wiser to give as little attention
as possible.

I told him to go to the light for education and healing.

# Northern Lights

One of  my  parents would wake me.
                         In a purposely, dim lit room.
Help me with shoes and coat.
Guid me gently out side

 Long transparent curtains of
                           rose, pink and blue
hung from the night sky. Other times constellations
pointed out.

Looking up, frightened me.
I felt myself going to the stars.
A hand on my shoulder   or
"Hold on to the wash line."

I stayed in my backyard.

A voice whispered.

"If you are ever lost out there.
Tell them you are from the Milky Way."

## A Call for Love        (age seven)

In the night, I woke.  he was rubbing
something hard along my back

Making low sounds in his through.
I lay motionless.
Eventually his movements slowed.
He stoped.
 Remaining still, holding my breath his
breathing changed.
I inched away, across the vast expanse of
mattress. Any sound from him, froze me in that
spot until he  was silent and still again.  Gradually
I eased myself across to the middle of the bed,
holding my breath while moving stoping to
breath. To the edge,  releasing my leaded weight
in slow motion.
Emptiness, filled me. I knew I would not be close to my
father ever again.
As I placing my hand on the cold, glass doorknob wishing
mom was home.
Terror swept through my body

*I'm safer alone.*

## My Favorite Cave

 the deepest chamber  make a fire
rattles and drum slow chant  my
body swaying to it's natural
rhythm   flames jump in hypnotic
shadows on the back wall dance
and sing, wild frantic frenzy biting
the lighting breath echoing
 On the cool ground my body expanding
stretching beyond the cave outside the
mountain into the universe my arm
extended  moon's face  is beside my
elbow

simultaneously my singe
cellular smallness
original cell first atom  heart
beating coming form within
the earth
 filling the chambers

until the mountain trembled.

## The Molding

And the mother father created
this girl child in their own image.

What I saw I did not see.
What I heard I did not hear.

My ears were their ears.
My eyes were their eyes. All
ideas were theirs.

My night mares were of trying to speak unable make sound

trying to walk, unable to move.

Not able to lift my arms to protect myself.

# River Severn

Between Wales and England.

River is speaking now. "I am furious."

Pushing and pulling; push pull  push pull
day and night  every day and every
night.

The wind against my flow, in my face *all the time.*

It is foolish to stand near any,  body

                              as enraged as I am.

## The Tree

I  saw an apple tree bare of its leaves It
was a sleep.

One apple died on the limb.

It did not know to let go.

## South Africa

I love to feel my mouth full of watermelon on
any summer morning.

Here we are in South Africa having breakfast.

Isabels mouth is stuffed with watermelon.

I can't feel a thing.

# Regrets

My cousin asleep on her living room floor.
Her husband, sat next to me on the sofa.
His hand on my breast.
Then between my legs.  What
did he want there?

I swear she was pretending to sleep. My
body went numb.

My heart felt as a fist pounding on the inside of my chest.

I sat motionless not moving even my eyes.

Breathing might encourage him.

I froze under his hand.

  Twenty years later I told my mom.

I want her to tell me how much she regretted not being
there.

She said "it was better for you, I was *not* there."


It would have been all my fault.

Parents House                                 My  Home

"My real parents will find me and take me home".

These are the only parents available to you for now.

A house of terror.

*My* home is filled  with peace and joy.

I do not answer. the door if both cats ran up stares


Maple seeds, helicopters twirling from limbs to the ground
all day and night. thee days whirling, a show.

The sun and moon rise and set in my bedroom windows.

Gaia knows my needs, to keep me healthy
                                    a thistle crop every year!

Now I  drive by, the spirit of the house calls to me.

"Please, come home!"

## Child Wife

Not a bride.

"Can I marry daddy?"

 The laughter of our relatives made the room shrink.

I was too large  there was no space for me,
                              in my parents  house.

If they had been   watching my dad. They

would have know the question was...

   More than Reasonable.

## The Royals

When in court.
    My sisters, brothers and myself

        remembered every thing spoken and seen. We

talked without saying anything,  admitted nothing.

we did not know or  remember;   when asked.

Our lives depended on it.

# Montsegur

It seemed as though I climbed most of the day.
 Sun on my back.   picked my  way through
the many pathways to the top to the chateau.
On my stomach Elbows and arms pulled
under the bushes for shade and rest.
The rocks were smooth, hot and slippery.
From all the knights, priests, tradesmen, and nuns who had
used these trails.
The last strong hold, of the Cathars,  against the Catholic
church. Choose the church or be corralled and burned alive.

Most of them jumped into the flames voluntary.

A woman holding on the bushes. Inside the path. facing the
mountain. She was crying and shaking,  her face and neck
were red.

Many times as a child had I known terror as this woman.
Too afraid to show it.
A release from my shoulders and  chest.

She was doing this for all of us

# A Shaman Drumming Circle

Carefully selected clothing.
Necklace and pouch.
Old friends, my favorite stones in pockets.
Wrapped drum in red cloth.
Three sessions of drumming.
Flying and weeping.
Faraway in outer space.
Looking back,  my tears spray in an ark.

Covering the Earth.

## Fools Rush In

An angel took me to a place told me
"This is Earth."
Take me away I want to stay.
Where *is* love free?
I need time to find my truth.
Teach me a language of kind words.
I want  gentleness.
If angles can't go there.

Someone has too.

Carl Sandburg; "You can't laugh off their capacity to take it.

Lightning Source UK Ltd.
Milton Keynes UK
UKHW011301170520
363416UK00003B/77/J

9 781984 578211